I0426509

TABLE OF CONTENTS

Book III

Book IV

This book is dedicated to the Arab world. It is not written to condemn. On the contrary, following the recent events in the Arab world, the dangers following a potential Third World War and the peace that is desired by the populous yet never offered by the leaders I decided to write this to inspire writers, philosophers and others of such professions to offer solutions. To attend to the matter of the ideal Arab State, and the methods in which it should be run in a secular fashion and offer solutions in a religious and political independent environment.

Preface

Many argue that the word Machiavelli has become synonymous
with deceit. I on the contrary believe that it is a realistic
approach to dealing with the society around you. Machiavelli,
much like Sun Tzu can be adopted in every aspect of one's life,
from politics to every day dealing with third parties.

Having an Egyptian father and a Greek mother I decided to
write. A thought is beyond politics, beyond society, beyond
known and unknown enemies and beyond boundaries. The
Arab world is the beginning yet as any individual of this society
I think. By thinking I live, I interpret; I reach conclusions,
participate in debates and argue my own points.

Thoughts on the Arab world are a contribution towards the
Arab populous, to Arab politics and my enlightener Niccolo
Machiavelli.

I can only acknowledge that some will agree and others not so
much but the point of this book is to enlighten those that can
disagree to create a discourse over the matter. By such
discourse this "THOUGHT" and all others that will accompany
it will spiritually enhance nations. Perhaps through that one can
finally witness the evolution of politics and international
relations from the ancient pause it has acquired.

There are numerous things Machiavellian thought can teach one
and as a Machiavellian author I intend to continue
Machiavelli's work and it's accuracy in today's world.

As the world is at its prime and international relations are an area that is based on ancient principles and applications of such principles in modernity, as well as the fact that there has been a progressive yet unstable growth of all sovereignties. The Arab world stands where Europe did thousands of years ago and that can only change if people stop caring for it. If there is political discussion, philosophical thought secularism, equanimity and lack of pressure of democratic adaptation.

What you, the reader will read from this point on isn't leftist, or rightist, nor does it associate itself with these two dogmas. I am no philosopher but I hold certain ideas that can help the Arab world.

My aim is not to adapt politics, but to evolve society.

Book One

I.   [THE BEST FORM OF GOVERNMENT]

Naturally there has been great controversy on the best form of government worthy of an Arab state. Primarily, when distinguishing what the best form of government is one must wonder what part of the map is considered an Arab state. For the purpose of this discourse I will focus only on Egypt, Libya, Lebanon, Morocco, Syria, Tunis, and Jordan as in my own opinion the aforementioned sovereign states and their role in modern world history have compelled me to write. Through them I saw what needed to be changed, how such sovereignties should be governed and all the social changes that that entails.

So what would the best form of government be in the states of Egypt, Libya, Lebanon, Morocco, Syria, Tunis, and Jordan? The war for worldwide 'democracy' has called the Western sovereignties to expect that the Arab states develop a western based model of government. Western democracy, whether a good or bad in practice is fundamentally based on the development of Western intellectuals, based on that was used to build the European model. Therefore in essence that cannot be applied in a state, a civilization that has a significant deviation from Western contemporary intellects. So what is it that Arab intellectuals state? Tahar Ben Jelloun had stated that: there are no Arab intellectuals of international stature because the Arab world lives in a state of generalized mediocrity. Jelloun clearly stated that the Arab world is suspended in a pit without touching the bottom of it.

Clearly then that is a sight of a beginning form of intellects, that automatically suspend themselves as they are prohibited from speaking, but like a divided house cannot stand, in effect a morally and intellectually divided state cannot state. To my great dismay then I cannot lead on discussing about an ideal form of government in an Arab Republic with solid examples and word of mouth spread via past philosophers, instead I must rely on my own initiative and imagination.

Primarily, the best form of government that will be chosen for the people, to serve the people is not based on ideologies but on principle. But this one should appreciate the leadership of the government his beliefs must not be scrutinized but his actions. In all societies and in particular Arab intertwined societies scrutiny is an approach well tied up with survival. To create a state that will stand tall like a strong tower instead of as Jelloun stated a broken house there must be a system of respect, discipline and appreciation from the citizen towards the leadership, from the leadership towards the citizen, religious leaders, and education.

Once there is a mutual system of respect, understanding, aiding and overall peace and the system of state that must be developed must decide on which way will they sustain the people. If the leadership consists of suspicious people that expect the civilian to cause havoc, then the nation state will be plunged with authority labelling it as a police state. And if such be the case then no Arab will be capable to express respect, nor respect the legal systems, and the authority. Hence no form of extreme police authority should be expressed upon the people. Though the Arabs differ from the Westerners if one thing is true for all nations, is that they express their true potential when extreme authority is not pressured upon them, or if so done, then the leadership should make sure it is done in far more discreet manners, much like the notorious intelligence services that exist in the Arab peninsula at the moment.

On more practical terms, the government should be based on an Egyptian model, where the parliament is elected in separate elections and are not tied in to particular parties, and then the Chancellor, President is elected on separated elections. However, I would personally suggest that an alteration to that would guarantee supreme tranquillity and excellence leadership in the Arab peninsula.

Firstly, I will base these words on the Aristotelian republic model. The virtuous and excellent should be placed under political institutions that enhance their excellence in politics, diplomacy and other forms of governance with the main goal being the successful creation of a united Arab state.

Democracy is a fantastic model of political usage. A model created and adopted by the west for the creation of a liberal and secular world in terms of domestic and international politics. However though such a system is adopted by the west it is impractical for the Arab world.

The Arab world has never been free, nor has it developed to a point where the populous can immediately place themselves in the phase of transition between ultimate dictatorship and democracy. Progressive growth leads to more sufficient outcome then what a complete transit would offer.

That is why the ideal transition of governments and the best form of government for the Arab world to adopt is based on secularist principles. The leaders of the Arab world should be preserved by international law to steadily ease a democratic system in the sovereignty. Until that is done secularism is the only method of transition to democracy. That method was used by the Christian world, The Western world, and that should be used by the Arab world.

Finally, the Arab world must make sure it maintains powerful relations, particularly through trade of products and or investments towards natural resources with other extremely powerful sovereign states. By nature that would mean the Russians and other Asian markets as the Arabs highly depend on the Russians for tourism, investments and protection. Though most of this sounds impossible to achieve, and probably is cause as humans we are all selfish and cannot live in a Utopian state, for such a state cannot be created it would be best not to demand a western based democracy onto the Arab world, and simply allow the nations to develop a Nasser like Unity with principles of the third universal theory which is based on a combination of democratic principles, and the much needed religious guidance of the Arab World.

On a note at this point I would like to state that in my own personal view of the matter there is not a right and accurate government that currently exists in theory or in practice that could be efficiently adopted in the Arab world, and thus through the use of secularism and freedom of governance the Arab world will inevitably create an appropriate government of its own.

II.   [RELIGION]

Religion comes with great controversy when addressing Arabs. The Christians and Muslims of the Arab world are extremely passionate with their religious beliefs, and because of that expanding into that matter must be exercised with extreme caution.

Numerous individuals argue that religion should be abolished. The Arab world has experienced a plethora of hardships since the dawn of Western religious cults which has led the Arab world itself be dependent on the connotation of religion. Such being the case religion would be highly recommended to be kept untouched but its effect minimized. As aforementioned there would be no scrutiny. This would give for example women their own choice of whether or not they should walk in public without a hijab. For those in charge of Islam claims that it is necessary but the exact words of the Quran do state:

"And tell the believing women to subdue their eyes, and maintain their chastity. They shall not reveal any parts of their bodies, except that which is necessary. They shall cover their chests, (with their Khimar) and shall not relax this code in the presence of other than their husbands, their fathers, the fathers of their husbands, their sons, the sons of their husbands, their brothers, the sons of their brothers, the sons of their sisters, other women, the male servants or employees whose sexual drive has been nullified, or the children who have not reached puberty. They shall not strike their feet when they walk in order to shake and reveal certain details of their bodies. All of you shall repent to GOD, O you believers, that you may succeed." 24:31

Furthermore science has taught us that women do have the same urges as men and must therefore be treated equally and like women must cover their chest men must cover the organs. If and due to the fact that there will be an extreme reaction to these words women decide that the hijab is necessary then I would suggest that men wear something similar as their hair might also be tempting the women. Both are equal in the eyes of Allah, God and the law and must be treated equally.

Religion though, as important as it is to the conscious of some, and must be kept alive for several more years before humanity evolves, history teaches us that it should not interfere with the state. Religion is there for the moral support and spiritual Enlightenment of the populous. This means that education should be a complete derivation from it, and so must be the government and the media. Religion should have a newspaper of its own, a channel of its own, a school of its own if requested but by no forms should intervene with the curriculum of the schools, and universities, foreign affairs, judicial factors and politics within the state.

Religion should strictly represent spirituality, and guidance. If it cannot offer people that and enforces with dictatorial means mainly due to lack of education their own prerequisites, then perhaps it would be wise for it to seize completely from existence.

As people do need it though, all representatives of religion in the Arab state should encompass a psychological test, an economic background check prior, during and after they commit to their service. Similarly with corrupted Elders, and Leaders, religious preachers who perform against the state should be trialled for the crime committed against the state, and against his people, and if found guilty should be stripped of all titles, condemned from all Arab states and deprived of retirement.

In my view then religion should be used the way it was used by Saladin himself. Lionheart was his enemy but that did not stop him from doing the right thing and helping Lionheart when he needed it. Above all we are humans and such barriers such as religion should not be there, they should be practiced and not pushing to extremes.

All Academics, Researchers, Scientists, Judges, civilians, Leaders and Elders, religious leaders that lead with virtue, or perform divine good for the people they should be honoured with Royal titles of protection for moral support, e.g. Sir, Duke, Lord, Protector, Honourable Member, Royal Dr., Lord master, etc . Such decisions on honorary titles would be made by a Council compromising of all members of all professions of the society in the particular sovereign state.

All in all, if religion needs to stay then it should stay, but it should be kept under severe control for it is easier for a man to betray his people in the Arabic world then to betray his God.

III.   [FROM COLONIES TO FREEDOM]

The Arab world has been subject to colonialism more than it has colonised itself. Arab's historically have originated as a Central Semitic group. Their expansion is due to the Muslim conquests of the 7th and 8th century. In modern history during the 13th century the Arab world was placed under the rule of the Ottoman empire and declined six to seven centuries later. At the end of world war one many European powers claimed colonial empire over the Arab world. British Mandate for Palestine, British Mandate of Mesopotamia, British protectorate of Egypt, French protectorate of Morocco, Italian Libya, French Tunisia, French Algeria, French Mandate of Syria and Lebanon and the so-called Trucial States, a British protectorate formedby the sheikhdoms on the former "Pirate Coast".

Naturally then, these states gained their independence after the Second World War, followed with eminent problems between the Arabs and the Israelis. Therefore their independence ended in theory in 1945, but with the rise of Arab nationalism, Western influence, religious oppression and nationalist extremes one can state with sufficient background knowledge that in theory the sovereignties of each and every Arab nation have remained under colonial influence.

Though the road to freedom might be long one fathoms that colonial oppression eventually subside par example the recent Arab rebellions taught the world that secular dictators are not accepted. That doesn't necessarily mean that those sovereignties have gained their total independence. Libya overthrew Gaddafi, and his visions of a United Arab front against the Western world, to replace him with Western based monetary system. Contradictory to that, in Egypt the revolution is still in process due mainly to the fact that their secular leader, Mubarak was replaced by a totalitarian nationalist who self-labelled himself as Pharaoh of the state. The grounds of Morsi's politics do not stand under Arab freedom, particularly when legislation is mixed with theology and politics. Why? Well when it is mixed you get a compilation of disasters such as the Vatican, Canon Law and the unjustified expeditions and death of thousands of innocent individuals.

Similarly, when you impose a Muslim fascist theology on a nation that has never been free but desires above all for once to gain its independence, and attempt to introduce Sharia Law, then by nature you will not have freedom, but instead self-impose, self-destruction between the fanatics, and the leftist liberals who desire above all the development of the sovereign state to a more free and secular nation.

Therefore, it is safe to say that the Arab world has never been free. It is hard to state when it will be free or under what circumstance it will be free but standard principles of realism must make us take into consideration that freedom might actually never come.

IV.   [CONTROVERSIAL ARAB LEADERS]

Perhaps to fully understand what an Arab leader in principle is, it would be appropriate to take a break here from modern leaders and venture a journey back into time of the crusades. ☐alā☐ al-DīnYūsufibnAyyūb known to the west as Saladin led the Islamic opposition against the Holy crusades in the Levant with a sultanate of Egypt, Syria, Mesopotamia, Hejaz, Yemen, and parts of North Africa. Now this man united the Muslims, and fought off the crusades but was also noted for his repeated noble and chivalrous behaviour which itself was noted by many Christian chroniclers who had gained respect for Saladin, including Richard the Lionheart. Saladin won the crusades in 1187 in the Battle of Haitin, and died in 1193 in Damascus as a poor man, having given all his wealth to the people. To clarify it then a controversial Arab leader then must be ultimately noble and chivalrous to his friends and his enemies alike, be able to unite his people, be generous and hold no profit for his own self, be capable to defeat the imperialists, and finally to have elements of socialist behaviour in his governance. That recipe guarantees as one will witness to create a fruitful controversial Arab leader.

Mahmoud Abbas had once called upon all Arabs and Muslims to visit Jerusalem in order to break the blockade imposed on Israeli and Palestinian soil, and help all local Arabs who faced harsh situations mainly due to the decrease of Arab visitors. His call was condemned by the plethora but one can witness that his call was a righteous one for his people. Surprisingly for some it would be just at this point to claim that the Arab world has had a fair-minded amount of leaders that have caused controversy across other civilizations.

Though, once Egyptian legacy might be flowing through the following words a note-worthy leader would be Gamal Abdel Nasser. Bright as Nasser might not have been in school, as he only spent forty-five days in high school when he was arrested and detained for political activism, Bueller his "torturer" got nothing from him. Nasser, now had united Sudan with Egypt, and even succeeded a short lived unity with Syria.

The Hero of the Soviet Union, the Order of Lenin survived assassination attempts and became the godfather of Arab nationalists even though Nasser himself implemented numerous socialist measures in an attempt to create a unique Pan-Arab socialism and the formation of a United Arab Republic via modernizations reforms in education, family law and imprisonment of those who created the civil war, the same people that today have lead Egypt to civil war. Proud as he was the defeat from the Israelis following the 1967's Six Days War led him to resign and three years later died from a heart attack following the conflict resolution of the PLO with Jordan.

So as much loves or hates socialism, religion and or modernization Nasser had managed to attack and unite all aspects of the Arab culture into one exceptional Union which though unsuccessful could easily be used by modern leaders to extend the legacy of that man.

Much like Nasser, Yasser Arafat was an inimitable and unique man. Noble and much controversial as men like them where hated by the west and loved by their own people which that alone creates a mysterious nobleness over their character.

Arafat survived an airplane crash into the Libyan Desert, and several more attempts until he was successfully poisoned by the Israelis. Much like Nasser, Arafat left school and took part in the combat in the Gaza area and fought alongside the Egyptian forces during the Suez Crisis. In the 1968 battle of Karameh Arafat ordered Fatah fighters (Fatah was the political party he had created) to hold their ground and fight the IDF attack. Such a bold and noble defence when facing death with your own eyes, against the greatest army that exists today led him win the battle and forced the Israelis to retreat. Much hated and loved, seen as liberator or as a religious lunatic that caused pointless havoc that is a matter that can be debated for eternity. However, one must note that if Arafat was a threat hence the infinite attempted assassinations. Now if a leader is so good and did well for the people then one must wonder why would the labelled "enemy," who claims to be righteous (also a matter that could be debated for eternity, for labels are labels) tried to kill him off so many times.

But perhaps the greatest controversy of them all is created by men such as Hussein, Bin Laden, Mubarak and Colonel Gaddafi. Colonel Gaddafi had a de facto sovereign rule of Libya for 42 years. Politically this man was an Arab Nationalist, and an Arab Socialist who governed the country according to his own way labelled as the third international theory, or Gaddafiism. In principle this theory was inspired by Islamic socialism, Arab nationalism, African nationalism and principles of direct democracy. Though I do not intend to propose what is right, and what is wrong the third universal theory stands opposite of Capitalism and Communism proposing a solution for the third world, and the much wounded Middle East. Gaddafi has been labelled by some a hero, who held grounds against

Western imperialism and by others as a dictator who violated Libyan people fundamental human rights. Gaddafi unlike the aforementioned with the exception of Saladin gave money to the people of Libya, with Libya holding a zero debt and a much valued currency, role in world politics, a keychain position in what would have become a united Arab front which would dominate oil markets, and one of the few countries in the world that did not have a Western based bank . Once the NTC got into power, following Gaddafis death, the first thing that was established was a Western bank.

Like most Arabs the influence of Gaddafi will never be known, whether positive or negative his name hangs with great controversy between the borderline of being both hated and loved.

The Arab World had and still has numerous leaders whose position stands without a clear cut description. Many of these men were bold, heroic and brave and many were cruel dictators who might or might not have loved their people. Men like Mohammad Rezza Shah Pahlavi the Shah of Iran, Qutuz, Omar al-Bashir, Khalil al-Wazir, Ali Abdullah Saleh, King Abdullah II of Jordan, Edward Said,Layla Khalid and numerous others are leaders, men and women, generals or not, leaders, philosophers, writers and doctors who are labelled to be both loved and hated, or hated and due to their caused death loved thereafter. Though impossible to retrieve these leaders from the past, impossible to chat with them about their plans, visions inspirations and dreams, one can only accept the controversy of their name and move one.

V.　　[INGRATITUDE AND TREASON]

It is a common fact to know that the populous remains ungrateful and is always likely to betray their leader with a minute promise by the enemy. A good leader is always taken for granted to cause benevolence whilst an evil leader is feared to cause death. That is why a good leader must be capable, in fear of ingratitude and treason to be capable of punishing those who betrayed him while maintaining peace, and making sure that they are not betrayed in the first place.

People are bound by nature to be filled with ingratitude and only proceed to respect their past leaders upon the dawn of a new leader who is by far worse than the past and the populous has regretted hating their past leaders. But when the past leader is worse than the present than the heart if the populous will be filled with even greater ingratitude for they will not appreciate their new leader and either label him as worse than the past or even show as much hate towards the new leader and for certain lead him to treason and potentially the destruction of the sovereign state.

In the view of the Romans then one punishment is deemed fit for treason and that is death. However, that is by far not the way of the Quran, and as we mentioned in the Arab world for the time being it is lucrative to maintain religion then death cannot be used as a form of punishment.

Imprisonment was used by controversial leaders to punish the ingratitude and treason by the populous. Nasser imprisoned most of the members of the Muslim Brotherhood to prevent a coup by a fascist theology. Mubarak did the same to such members. However in the case of the most recent Arab leaders, like Gaddafi, Mubarak and Assad there is great controversy over their punishments. Word of mouth states that they used high quality torture methods like chemical weapons and torture of the traitors in the deserts.

Now the question that rises is whether such forms of punishment should be valid in the twenty-first century. First, without any form of foreign intervention there would be no uprisings in the Arab world, therefore their methods were interiorly successful, but illegitimate on two grounds:

Primarily, such methods used violate the religious principles on which the Arab world stands, and since we stated that the Arab world as we mentioned needs religion then we must stand on the grounds that the leaders should practice what they preach.

Moreover, it is clear cut that such attitude is offensive and violation of the fundamental human rights of the Arabs. So then we must respect international laws and not kill for treason and ingratitude.

As we have established then that death is not a fathomed measure of punishment then alternatives must be found.

Perhaps then the safest and most accurate measure that can be taken to prevent the populous from performing their ingratitude and preventing their treason we must take the occupied Palestinian territory and perform similar punishments. Primarily then exile and declined return to their homeland must be a form of punishment. Being in exile can only make one wiser in many ways and the form of exiles that can be formed upon the betrayal of the masses can be many, like exile from homeland, their home, and or other privileges of a society. To secure lack of treason exile must be performed on a few in order to teach the many as has been done always. The Roman army used to sentence to death some generals to prevent the treason by the rest.

I firmly believe that death is not applicable, but exile can be a solution, though in today's intertwined world it would be of greater sufficient to remove privileges of society. For Arabs are noteworthy of performing deeds which enhance their names in the social structure, and by removing that for charges of treason and or lack of social care will by nature reduce them on the social structure and thus prevent such further actions. Therefore to prevent ingratitude and treason one must thus punish through social or factual exile the masses that performed such unconstitutional acts against the state.

VI.   [USE AND ABUSE OF DICTATORSHIP]

The use and abuse of a dictatorship is quite a touchy subject when it comes to the Arab world. As I have aforementioned it is quite clear that the Arab world has never separated itself from forms of dictatorships and progressed to a republic or a western approached democracy. Therefore to establish what an abused dictatorship in the Arab world I will clearly reach the following conclusion that all forms of dictatorship, all and every kind have been established by the need of the Arab world to establish freedom. Because in due time it all comes down to the following fact that the harder the people struggle for freedom the harder they will be surprised by their revolutionary leaders.

The use of dictatorship in the Arab world in my own view is hereto justified to a certain extend. If the republic must be found upon a dictatorship then it is for certain then that a secular dictatorship is much more appropriate then a fascist theology found upon lack of rightfully chosen leaders which falsely lead against the secular government which uses dictatorship to control the populous. The populous which as stated holds the same mentality and religious dependency of the western world did a century ago.

Now then since a form of dictatorship must be used the line must be drawn to where it is abused. Abused dictatorship would then be in its finest example President Morsi of Egypt, or the expansion movements of the Israeli government against their own people. The line is drawn between a just use of dictatorship and abuse of dictatorship when leaders became so anti-secular that two religious opponents that originated from the same bloodline hold hatred for so long.

The abuse of dictatorship is found when after the struggle of the masses the populous is brainwashed into believing that Sharia law is a just method of ruling.

So to satisfy all prior thoughts secular dictatorship is an unwanted yet needed method, if used correctly. But when it turns to abuse of the power then for all republics sake it must be prevented at all cost.

Dictatorship and strong dictatorship is particularly visible in the UAE, Saudis Arabia and generally that part of the region. It would be strong to state that that economically beneficial and governmentally strong dictatorship is not but a mere example of treason towards all Arabs. Therefore I will in essence tackle the issue of that Dictatorship and the populous.

Many may find themselves happy in that region of the world. However the populous that is well educated and resides in that area along with Western populations strongly scrutinize the government and the Sharia Muslim extremist religious beliefs. As proxies states in case of Middle East warfare they are not condemned for their actions by strong sovereignties such as the USA. However, on a social scale it lacks the support a secular government needs to allow progression within their nation state. In essence then these powers remain nothing but soft powers with strong economies. There is great potential to evolve to a Smart power that uses the combination of the stick and the carrot, with strong regional control and support. If leadership decides to serve the people it is clear that such states can progress without the need of western allies yet with western support. It is as simple as abolishing the murder of women who have been raped, the punishment of fathers who beat their children and a minimisation of religious corruption.

VII.   [MANAGING THE POPULOUS]

The populous in an Arab Republic are by all means a dangerous lot.
The devotion to religion is stronger than the populous devotion to
one's own selves and family. The role of the family is just as
significant but nevertheless to manage such a populous a just leader
must be capable of manipulating their values as their own and preserve
a simple status quo parallel to the status quo of the masses.

The populous then in the Arab world must fear the leaders and the
punishments of one's faulty behaviour. Therefore, for the populous to
remain stealthy there must be a strong maintained force, a strong
police force with a fierce appearance, not with the power to
malevolently punish the misbehaving masses, but appear to be as such
fierce in order to maintain tranquillity. The laws then must be upheld
with no exception, whether broken by the leaders or the populous, and
the punishments must never over exaggerate the crime that was
committed.

But do not get these words wrong, for these words are synonymous to
a dictatorship. I must entail here that once more the Arab world has
virtually never been free, and the progression to a free state must be
done partially, why? Direct access to a Southern European style
freedom will inevitably lead the populous to distinct corruption and
misbehaviour.

The populous must be aware of the intentions of the state. In my own opinion then the populous must be treated equally and know the full truth and intention of their sovereign state but in order for the state to be maintained and the populous managed it must be accurate that you can never walk alone. Set the values and principles of the state parallel to the values and principles of the populous: family, honour, dignity, to an extend religion, and above all education.

There is no righteous set of principles one can identify in order to govern such a country and maintain the populous, but what I suggest as an overall key behaviour is to provide a wealthy life for the populous for the masses like to live in wealth and are more keen to forget the loss of their mother then the loss of their fortune. Through such preservation of fortune the populous will remain loyal. One must only look at Dubai, Saudi Arabia, Kuwait and all such wealthy nations to realize that to manage the populous in the Arab world one needs a wealthy populous and an intimidating police force.

But once more like I aforementioned in my previous work, much like the appropriate government needed for the Arab world the question of how to manage the populous is a question that can only be answered efficiently only in progress and process of the Arab World.

Book Two

I.   [METHODS OF PRESERVING PEACE]

Peace is another controversial topic of discussion when it comes to the sovereignty of an Arab state. Like all Arab states have never been free, it is only rational to then assume that they have never been in peace is as well. From the Sultanate from Turkey fought by many Arab nations for their independence to the revolt against the British by Iraw and Egypt, the Franco Syrian war, to the Palestinian riots of 1929 to the Simele massacre, Ararat Rebellion, the White Revolution, the Jordan-Palestinian Civil War, the Lebanese Civil War and the Arab world keeps counting. The question is then how to create, maintain and preserve peace.

Primarily, to create peace considering the recent revolutions in Egypt, Syria, and Libya, I will clarify that in order to create peace at this current time The answer is simple. If anyone reads back to the history of Islamic Extremism, we could see that it all started by the USA funding and arming the Talibans and other Extremist Islamists in different regions of the Muslim World to fight against Communism and the USSR, for example in Afghanistan. Which means the Talibans and Extremist Islamists are nothing more than puppets of the USA rooted in Countries of the Muslim World to cause Conflicts and ruin the development of the Arab World into Secularism. On the other hand, the Russian Leader Putin which is supporting Secularism in those Regions. Russia a Country that has fought against Islamic

Terrorism in its own territory, like Chechnya knows very well that Islamic Extremism is a disease created and rooted by the USA. The Americans have used this puppet against the Russians once in Afghanistan, Putin is not willing to let it happen for the second time.

Now let's come to Egypt. We all know about the coup by the Egyptian Military which overthrew the Islamist Government in Egypt by the Muslim Brotherhood. The West is trying to convince us that the coup d'etat was an action against Democracy. That's very ironic, the Muslim Brotherhood a Democratic Party? A Party with a Sharia Law agenda is nothing related to peace and its core of Secularism. The Egyptian Military only wants to secure the Egyptian Society with Religious Freedom and Secularism, in order after words to move on to a peaceful transition to Democracy. Once again though the West is fanatically against it and the question that should be asked is why? Just like I mentioned before about Syria, Islamist Extremism is the puppet of the USA rooted into Countries to prevent their development for Political and Geostrategical reasons, for example Isarels role in the Region and its strong alliance with the USA. Turkey, since it was founded by the Secular Pro-Western leader Mustafa Kemal Ataturk has had a society and policy of Secularism. For the past decade this Country has been ruled by an Islamist, Turkish Prime Minister Recep Tayyip Erdogan which has long been flirting with the Muslim Brotherhood. His aim is to rise as the new Ottoman Islamic leader of the Region, by making Turkey the Islamic Regional Power of the Muslim World. Only way to do so is by funding the Muslim Brotherhood in Egypt and other

Islamic Extremists in other areas of the Region which are sympathetic with his view of how the Region should be.

The Conclusion for me is that, the only way for the Arab and Muslim World to reach anywhere close to a peaceful system is by having Secular Totalitarian Leaders, in order to prevent Islamic Extremists from having any space to rise in power. Then those Countries can have a transition process to permanent peace through an unfortunate progressive growth via Secularism and education.

Not only that, to establish a peaceful region where the Arabs would unite, where growth would be progressive yet successful one should apply a formula based on an equilibrist tuned balance of power in the following way: An economically powerful but militarily weak Arab state should alliance with a militarily powerful Arab state which is economically weak and vice versa, that way all edges are covered and there is a progressive growth of all states simultaneously. Since on the international level such states still cannot compare with powers such as the Saudis or other superpowers I would also like to propose a shift of support from the states from a pro West stance to a strictly business terms with the west and strong alliances with the East. Thus underdeveloped countries would progress quicker and balance the power of the Western world.

A peaceful sovereignty state should always keep in mind that war is an option and therefore alliances should always be formed to dominate over a swift battle with other potential enemies without in any way or form be instigating any form of negativity and continuous hatred cause with such manner peace will never be created or preserved.

II.   [DIPLOMACY AND WAR]

As was aforementioned war should be prevented at all cost, therefore the diplomats of an Arab nation must look in an alternative method of diplomacy. Rival superpowers should be stabilized with the nation state of the diplomat. Economic ties must be created between the superpowers and the state in such a manner that when time is needed the superpowers will have to act in a fashion of benefit to the Arab state.

That being said warfare has many forms which will be explained further later, economic, interior, exterior, spiritual, educational, and The Coup of the people. Economic warfare is perhaps the most significant of all because through the use of the first all the others can be instigated. Economic warfare can be in forms of embargos, tax evasion, and force to join international monetary institutions and/or the creations of Westernized Banks in the Arab State.

The diplomats of that state should therefore tie foreign interests to the Arab State to the extent that economic warfare would for most certain be of privilege to foreign powers. However to prevent that economic warfare it would be highly suggested that through a number of unforeseen tricks the Arab state should be capable of holding significant economic power and funds be able to influence the decisions of foreign leaders to cause warfare. To enhance that it would be highly suggested that natural resources be used to tie high powered companies with the Arab state. Through the use of diplomatic measures, economic equilibrium should be created to prevent the use and abuse the profit of the foreign investment funds. In such a manner it would be sufficient to the profit of the Arab state and prevention of economic warfare.

Diplomacy must then be used to prevent interior war as well. Interior warfare is perhaps the most dangerous method of war. It usually involves ambitious leaders designed to overtake the Arab sovereignty. Usually such movements are illegal by international law but through a series of incognito moves funded by international organizations and/ or superpower sovereign states. Such examples are vast in international history, movements such as that by the CIA and the United Fruit Company in Latin America, and more recently the Muslim brotherhood knowingly funded by Turkey and many other such states. Diplomacy must then be used with such dangerous powers and potential enemies of the state. Primarily this should be guaranteed through a twofold manner:

Primarily, the Arab state that wants to prevent interior struggle and fighting must have the populous on its side, thus being able to fund for a good quality of life for the masses. That way the masses will be reluctant to join such groups and will remain loyal to the leadership. That can also be further enhanced through the creation of public offices and other such where the leadership appears close to the masses and the popular belief of the populous is such that they feel loyal to their leaders.

Secondly, there must be at least and iconic image of liberation and control over potential states that might engage in such a behaviour. That can be created as aforementioned by economic ties and or clear cut diplomacy where it is publicly stated that such policies will lead to war. Therefore in such cases it is wiser to prevent war via warfare then to bring the state on the verge of civil war as is Egypt today.

There are a consortium of things that one could further mention on the matter. The Arab world is fragile and warfare has been everlasting. The exterior methods of warfare an Arab world can encounter are through businesses, paramilitary troops and funding of extremist organizations that could lead for the worse of the sovereignty of the state if they are allowed into government position or if they have enough arms which inevitably will result in civil war.

Spiritual warfare and educational warfare are very much alike. Powerful as they are, in their own essence, and successful in their own way by fundamentally attacking the conscience of the populous, and more precisely those who are religious and children through their education and their beliefs. Spiritual warfare is using the belief of Islam in this case to either cause a distinct difference between the sexes and/or to create a justifiable manner of valorous hate towards other religions and civilizations.

The righteous diplomat and ministerial servant must be clear aware of their enemies which are virtually every other state where interests may be crossed. The ministerial servants must be aware of the motifs, aware of the possible outcomes and be ready to adjust and fight on all levels of invasion. Just like that they must also be able to maintain a successful upper hand on all conditions to prevent any manner that might harm the state.

III.   [ADMINISTRATION OF THE EXPANSIONISTS]

The administration of any expansionist during the time of the invasion will often be labelled democratic, whilst yours dictatorial. The administration will always be labelled free while the Arab Worlds will always be labelled an imprisonment.

Political philosophy as easy as it can be to the reader it is quite hard to guess. The administration of any expansionist though during the course of history has been the same. The formula is such:

Create an enemy+ his refusal to grant you economic benefit+ creation of an act of terrorism/ or a violation of human rights = a just cause to invade with full support by the expansionists populous

Further than that, as much as it seems democratic the governance of the populous of the expansionist state would be the ones living in a state of fascism over that of liberty offered.

Now knowing the Arab world the least that can occur in the Arab world with such an agenda by the expansionists' civil and actual warfare appears inevitable.

The administrations of the expansionists won't be different to that of the expansionism of let us say The Crusaders thousands of years ago, for and sole purpose of invasion. Land, oil, money and other such is enough to achieve full purpose of cover up of the expansionist administration to justify an invasion.

On this matter there is nothing further that could be said, nor wished for other, than for the populous to believe no word from what is being stated but to dream, expect and study the history books of the past that show the true face of expansionism.

As long as any Arab nation is capable of defending itself through arms, and through dialogue(again much like Assad) they will be capable of defending the sovereignty of their nation.

On the contrary if they are as gullible as Morsi or Mubarak where the whole of the country ran on the administration of the foreign occupiers than it is rational that they fall and that the administration of the expansionist comes to life and in this case is the reason of havoc in the overall state.

The expansionist's administrations can be highly dogmatically successful in achieving its aims.

In Gadhafi's case the very fact that foreign assassins and missionaries where hired In order to fight the rebels and their foreign troops was a mistake that cost Gadhafi, Libya and the expansionist another fallen sovereignty that would serve their purposes.

Thus any foreign administration that is fought should be fought by all means by one sovereignties own power and her allies. Never, but never should there be any foreign hired troops for they can easily change sides and ally with the expansionist as well as sell their leader, employer, payer inevitably at any time. Most importantly though such individuals do not feel pain for the land they are fighting for and thus fight only half-heartedly. Why? Cause there aim is not to protect their homeland but to ensure a pay check.

IV.   [MISTAKES CONNECTED WITH WAR]

Perhaps the most notorious mistake connected with war is the isolation of the potentially defeated nation. An Arab Republic during times of war has been noted to isolate itself from alliances within states. The Arabs perhaps out of pride or perhaps due to lack of strategic leadership refuse to seek help from other nations and isolate themselves completely from nations with different principles, mainly religious.

For example, with the current uprisings, the Arab world shows distaste to the West, righteously or falsely that is an irrelevant matter for the politics of the inner state as an enemy can be an enemy despite the potential aid that may be offered during war.

The primary mistake I can connect then with the Arab state during war is isolation. If you notice the actions of the leadership it is perhaps done out of pride for the past hatreds between foreign governments. The populous is not one to easily erase a grudge for a foreign government particularly if that grudge holds a history of war, violence and deceit. But in order to come out victories from war the Arab nation under attack must form alliances that would be difficult to fathom prior to war. To ensure victory and prevent mistakes such as civil war, death of innocent populous, children, terrorist and others it would be safe to secure alliances.

For example one can look at Palestine. Following the British Mandate and the partition of the Palestinian state, Palestinian leaders where too late in asking for help and from the wrong sovereignties at the time, it was practically a war that was already lost from the start.

Why? Well from personal experience in my sovereign mind it would have been wiser to follow international procedures whilst also attempting alliance with foreign powers such as Russia, China, Japan, and Turkey. As surprising as that may sound the Palestinian nation at that time could have had a sturdy spine to hold them up against internationalism and pretty much occupation. Thus when the Arabs went into war against the Israelis they would have done so with an army as powerful if not even more powerful than the Western based Israeli. If there were economic ties, then the war would have been won and Israel could have possible now been a peaceful state where citizens from all religions could be able to live harmoniously.

Religion is so important to the Arabs and the Israelis, as much as it is to the Russians, Turks, Greeks and Italians. Through that and with a different approach I can firmly say that piece of holy land could now have been in peace.

But in order to ensure a successful alliance and prevent abusive behaviour from the aiding sovereignty in the future, which would be a worse mistake in the future it would also be wise that the Arab world bonded themselves economically with the aiding state. In war, frantically everything is allowed, but if the aiding state is economically tied to the attacked nation it would have no option but to help, just as it would have no further option of aiding the populous and be incapable of influencing the Arab government latter.

A further mistake that can be connected with war is religion, particularly in an Arab state. Religion can force the Arab state into alliances with states that hold the same religious baselines and that can be significantly wrong due to the fact that not only does it prevent political secularism in the state but the fact that the results of most wars could be similar to that of Palestine, in pure defeat.

Fundamentally then the mistakes noticed in the Arab world are:

Pride, in refusing to see potential aid from other non-Arabs in times of war and peace.

Lack of leadership, for right leadership could acknowledge where aid can come from, and would know how to fight off any enemy on any ground and under any terms.

Ignorance, as the Arabs refuse to trade victory with economic benefits from foreign companies.

Finally, I believe the Arab world lacks the determination to win. The Arab world has never been truly united as one to fight an enemy off. Perhaps before talking about mistakes in war it would be wise to see them united and ready to fight off an enemy as one nation, one heart, and one soul.

V.   [DEALING WITH NEIGHBOURS IN WAR]

As was aforementioned alliances with foreign powers should be secured during war. Prior to that though, one must look at the role of the neighbouring states. During the recent uprisings in Egypt, Qatar found an opportunity to fund the extremists in return to Egyptian artifacts. Similarly, Saudi Arabia is pro to an attack towards Assad in Syria. Therefore, in order to deal with thy neighbour in war, the primary move would be to understand the aims and purposes of their policies and course of action.

For if the neighbouring sovereignty is a friend then the Arab state must ensure to strengthen that friendship in order to be provided with an extra line of defence in case of war. Here it would be wise to state that always in such cases an eye must be kept open because the behaviour of states is much similar to the course of action of humans. They may promise friendship, protection and aid in times of war but could with no guilt of conscience bend towards the higher bidder and betray their promise. It would be wise for the Arab state to ensure if not aid at least the neutrality of the neighbouring state in war. How? Again the wisest method in my view would be through economic ties. Acknowledging though that that may be impossible what would be further suggest is via a number of diplomatic coups ensure the neighbours neutrality by using a more powerful if not a supra state on your side. From fear, that ought to be sufficient and enough to maintain the neutrality of thy neighbour, but what if it isn't?

In case it isn't, and the neighbour of a centred Arab state is an enemy or even a potential threat the Arab should use methods mastered to ensure a Blitz style victory.

That can only be ensured via one successful manner. Primarily every Arab nation should have a secret paramilitary unit large enough and enormously well trained that could ensure victory when used against the enemy, a certain unit of super soldiers if one would like. When, in warfare State X feels that her neighbour, State Y might be in agreement with State X's enemy and might potentially harm State X, State X must deploy these super soldier unit in secrecy to ensure the neutrality of State Y.

The paramilitary unit must be composed of young and cunning men, who through the use of siege warfare as well as psychological warfare would be capable to erase the potential threat. For example, Alexander would leave a few samples lying around the scene of his victories. After he had gone Persians would find this armour and were soon spreading stories of Alexander's superhuman giant soldiers. A modern alteration of that could be the use of religion. Through continuous psychological warfare and arms war and by creating a number of enmities that show that Allah is on their side, the paramilitary would be able to scare off a cast majority of the populous thus creating a lack of support for the governments' potential attack. Furthermore, such actions would demoralize the troops themselves and even if the neighbouring state did declare war, the soldiers would be in such fear of the wrath they might experience that victory would be swift and efficient.

In conclusion then to deal with a neighbour in war an Arab state has three possible courses of actions:

- Make friends with the neighbouring state and promise in case of aid economic, arms and other such forms of deals.

- Expect aid, make friends yet be potentially aware of betrayal, therefore using another more powerful sovereignty as a backbone to indirectly threaten your neighbour to remain inactive during your war.

- Through the use of paramilitary weaken your enemy by causing internal problems making them a weak enemy, and a powerful territorial shield.

Book Three

I.   [REFORM, SECURITY AND THE ELIMINATION OF RIVALS]

Reform is defined as:To improve by alteration, correction of error, or removal of defects; put into a better form or condition. Thus reform, the correction of error should be tied to security, and security to rivals. Therefore with the title of the first section of the third book the results should be that in an Arab republic all governmental and security reforms should be done to abolish a rival.

As was aforementioned the Arab world needs secular dictatorship to steadily progress to a democratic, liberal state, assuming that a Western based Democracy is the right governance for the Arabs. Change though is a continuous process and as that change occurs it would be wiser for one to experience a moment in the future then to live an eternity in the past. That is the only thing that I can say in confidence and through that the train of thoughts that follows is to eliminate past rivalry so thus complete wipe out any form of rivalry in the region and then precede to the reforms and further security enhancements.

One must add that this is a tricky business. At this point I would like to insert to notorious quotes which I will use later on but I am adding them now so they exist in my train of thoughts:

A democracy cannot exist as a permanent form of government. It can only exist until the voters discover that they can vote themselves money from the Public Treasury. From that moment on, the majority always votes for the candidate promising the most benefits from the Public Treasury with the result that a democracy always collapses over loose fiscal policy always followed by dictatorship.

- Alexander Fraser Tyler,'The Decline and Fall of the Athenian Republic'.

The second quote I would like to add is:

"If the Arabs put down their weapons today, there would be no more violence. If the Jews put down their weapons today, there would be nomore Israel'"

— Benjamin Netanyahu

From this point on I would like to proceed with primarily tackling reform. Once the founders and creators of democracy established that as a governing functional it serves for a minute time frame and not for the consortium of the health of the populous as it builds popularity on the common ideology of greed plus what I aforementioned that the Arab world should permit philosopher kings to provoke the spread of a new Arab based ideology that combines all Western ideological mistakes and combusts them permitting the growth of a third way of governance.

I cannot provide the solution for this third way for I am no king, no philosopher nor do I have the mental capability to identify hidden flaws and use these flaws to create brand new governance. Therefore, all the following reforms are natural reforms that I find fit to be part of any Arab society despite of its governing body.

Primarily, reforms should be found in schools. The educational system must be enhanced. The Arab world, along with Greece and Italy, a matter to discuss on other books should have had the most powerful educational facilities of the world. Therefore the syllabus must become more liberal towards science, tougher, harder in order to push students to the limits, thus creating well educated high school graduates that are capable of coping with the outside world. Stating that I believe that the connotation of University should be completely deviated from high school, because it is one's conscious choice that makes him want to go to university, and thus that cannot be predetermined by the behaviour of third parties in his high school.

Such reform will bring a more secular, and liberal approach to society, politics and religious matters. And ones that is achieved I believe it would only be a matter of time before secular dictatorship evolves into something greater for the Arab world, and only then I believe they will be able to enhance their political stability.

Enhancement of political stability ultimately vigorously places the question of interior and exterior security. This is where the second quote ties up.

The Arab world is then placed to a dilemma. Free from social bonds and having evolved into a new religiously, socially and politically liberal era still have to face their rivals, which is not only Israel in this case but many Arab countries as well who have chosen to side with Western powers instead of aiding their own people.

Now the first side of the coin dictates war with your enemies via the use of your new allies and liberal society which could attract western interest. In that case the Arab world would be facing a massacre, genocide on both sides with a second wave of rising extremism and the result being plunging the Arab world in further years of havoc.

Or there could be economic and social bondage. Money ties the world up and once societies who are sworn enemies have profit from one another they ultimately will become friendlier and thus solve all problems via democratic methodologies which would eventually entail a new creation of Arab secular unity against predetermined dogmatic principles adopted.

In a few words with effective secular reforms and successful diplomatic relations the Arab world will increase its territorial security and will be able to create and sustain long term peace with no forms of rivalry with its states. Thus through effective diplomacy and education defined by secularism perhaps stability can be created in the Middle East. And stability itself will then create a territorial Union over powered and with the ability to command and kneel any potential rivalries and enemies of the state.

II.   [OPPOSING POLITICAL IDEOLOGIES]

An Arab sovereignty can face numerous problems in its reformation to a secular political system particularly in the form of political ideologies. Modern era has encountered the creation of a new lethal ideology. Some call it extremism, others fanatics but for the purposes of thoughts I would like to give it a clearer definition. The political system that has emerged in Egypt via the Muslim brotherhood which entails the same rebels as the ones in Libya, Lebanon and the Syrians which are funded as aforementioned by Turkey is far beyond extremist. In my own mind I can only identify it as a far right western sponsored theological fascism. This new political ideology uses violence to create means and justify actions. There are however, numerous potentially opposing political ideologies that can be potentially witnessed in an Arab state.

Primarily, theological political expansionism, a political ideology that entails the church or other such religious houses and meddle with the sovereignty by placing pressure on omens and beliefs to achieve means. Those means could be expansionist movements, warfare, or massive populous brainwashing. Such political ideologies that are placed on the far angle of the right wing and extremist religious beliefs should be the priority of the state to exonerate.

Similarly in a secular state where progression should be done in a steadfast manner there should be secular political parties. Once more it is impossible to expect political and economic growth in a secular fashion if there is influence from Western political ideologies. As a matter of fact there can't be any secular growth if there is any political influence.

Thus the secular leader should not have influenced political parties, nor should such be permitted. Instead there should be cooperation between secular and non-secular Arab states with the educated young elites, that being students of philosophy, politics, literature and economics so that these states could create their own political ideologies which is based on the needs of the Arab world.

In a democracy opposing political ideologies and so would they be in a free and open society. It is compelling that political rivalries will be permitted in a secular society that attempts to progress to freedom.

As long as rivalry is based on the truth and legal methods of arguments on both sides then it is for the populous to decide who to believe and who to follow.

All political groups should be attempting to result the same outcome, The creation of a united Arab state that is supernatural and super economically powerful. Their methodologies should be different and in case extremism appears there should be hidden products of the system that have been given birth to destroy dictatorship.

Dictatorship is natural to the Arabs. Much like the line of Adam Smith to the Rothschild's the Arabs have never kept peace and freedom for long, and that is the only thing that should be preserved under any circumstances.

Opposing political ideologies are very dangerous for a state that wants to progress, particularly in its prime for it can cause extremities and plunge the state into decades of war, fanatics, extremist politics, civil war and other such malevolent havoc.

Democracy as a constitution dictates that opposing political ideologies exist. And for those purposes I will agree as well. However I will this liberality to parties and ideologies that exist within the constitutional rainbow and declare that far right fascist, far left and religious extremist ideologies should be prevented and their members prosecuted.

III. [ON CONSPIRACIES]

Humanity in its past years of life has come across numerous conspiracies. Conspiracies such as the twin tower attack, the Masonry, the Assassins, Religion, society, economics and so forth. I will not discuss the validity or not of such conspiracies but instead I will attempt to deal with how an Arab sovereignty can deal with a conspiracy threat against the creation of a free society.

This section is dedicated to the champagne drinking uranium depleting suit wearing killers. Power is a drug and the rest of the world will feed the addiction, for the colonizers and unjust warfare to achieve economic benefit from the Arabs.

When an Arab sovereignty comes against a conspiracy it should be perceived as a direct threat to the state permitted it is actually a negative conspiracy.

For example, if there is word of mouth that USA intends to bring democracy to Libya, Libya should directly mobilize, inform her allies and bring the matter to her acknowledgment as well as in the essential presence of the Western world and the international organizations in charge.

Arabs need freedom, and they do not know freedom the way the West knows it, if one argues that what we have is freedom. Because of that I will say from the bottom of my heart that it is for the best of the populous if they fight foreign interventions in any form or way even if such intervention is spread through conspiracies then to do nothing and plunge back to right wing, religious dictatorial darkness.

We all deserve life in this world we are living in and because of that it is irrelevant whether or not mobilization is necessary. For another sovereignty will think twice and even respect your demand for lack of foreign intervention if it witnesses a nation, a unity of nations that are ready to fight even against the rumour of intervention.

Conspiracies should be prevented at all cost. The secular government should promote discussions and any inner and underground civil un rest that could harm the outcome of secularism should be dealt with without violence but with discussions and goal sharing.

To this point then I would like to state that it is for the best of the sovereignty to deal the problems within the unity of the Arabs with interstate and inter sovereignties discussions instead of using violence. On the contrary when it comes to foreign conspiracies direct and necessary action should be adopted to prevent such conspiracies from coming to life.

Any other form of known conspiracies, and conspiracy groups should be banned and punished. Such conspiracy groups are lethal to the state. They create menace, influence politics and usually serve foreign agendas, or even their own profitable agendas. Thus I will persist on this point that foreign conspiracy groups that irrelevant of how they are named, charity foundations or whatever you name it be prevent from being created, or if created kept under strict control.

Social and educational conspiracies on the other hand should be always permitted. From such one can fathom that the purpose of freedom and secularity is consistently growing. If reforms are asked, and if such conspiracy groups demand reforms the government should grant such reforms. Through conspiracies on education and social life AND via the control of such from a secular sector the populous will only drastically progress to the liberality needed.

One conspiracy theory well known to the masses is that most governments are arms and drug dealers. Whether or not such theories are true is not the purpose of this work. On this point I shall warn that I will be very right wing strict and condemning.

If the Arabs want a secular and healthy society, despite its alliances, economic benefits or any other form of outcome that may lead from such business the Arab world should be capable and catch any drug dealing and drug transportation. Punishments should also be strict for any cargo that contains such drugs as well as severe punishment for local inner state drug and arms dealers.

Through that, and in particularly if the Sovereign Union of Arabs become aware that it is another sovereign entity that is behind such international money laundering and drug dealing the Arabs must make sure they embargo the nation that is in charge in any form or way particularly through the oil and food business as well as through the

Suez. Then the Arabs must make sure to bring the matter to the attention of international law so that that state is in fact punished.

I remain strong on that opinion as that will enhance the tolerance of social boundaries, higher public condemnation and a final solution to the international drug problem.

Not to mention the fact that it will create trust towards the Arabs as a safe yet liberal environment. If education is enhanced the Arab world could then easily become the centre of the world for education, where anyone could study in relative peace

V.   [ADAPTATION OF THE GOVERNMENT]

Sparta created laws and lived happily with her laws for over then eight hundred years. On the contrary a state that was unhappy was one that fell on the hands of corrupted and diseased legislators. A government that will never hence need to adapt will be of a combination of three powers, the people, the nobles, and the leaders and their legislation. Perfection will be reached if there is a balance of the Senate and the populous.

As a tribute to my personal mentor I would at this point like to state that the government should then be Machiavellian based, and such means combine a cunning, deceptive , and deceitful kind of resourcefulness in its participation, debates, foreign and inner policies and its civil excellence. That in turn allows the state to adapt to all forms of circumstances that might in essence influence her.

All forms of ineffectual bickering, a phenomenon quite transparent with the Arabs should be disillusioned and thus the rulers should be willing to set aside ethical concerns of justice, honesty, and kindness in order to maintain the stability of the state or that of the Arab union as a whole.

Julius Caesar had once stated that: Men willingly believe what they wish to be true. Therefore the Arab government should not deviate from its secular purpose under any circumstances. If necessary it should appear to do so and further then that it should be able to adapt to the circumstances. In essence then they should not allow their yesterday to represent much of their today, and if that means adjusting to a new era of proxy politics then by all means they should.

Before I continue, I would like to clarify what the term proxy politics is. In accordance with my thought proxy politics are political measure taken from a prime sovereignty towards another via a third sovereignty or international body. This can be witnessed through the US condemnation of Assad and Assad's response to the challenge imposed. Assad is therefore adapting to proxy politics but maintaining sovereignty over his state.

It would be ideal if adaptation only took form of politics, social and education. However since we do not live in the Machiavellian era, this might be profoundly impossible. The government then should have the mental ability and educated diplomats and other government officials to proceed from a secularist society to a social democratic or liberal society. Adaptation to such should inevitably be done in due time. Circumstances might call for preliminary actions to be taken from the government of the sovereignty and it should always be prepared to do so.

A fine example of adaptation would be that of the world to the challenge of climate change.

Here I would like to further insert a quote;

The greater the state, the more wrong and cruel its patriotism, and the greater is the sum of suffering upon which its power is founded.

Leo Tolstoy

Not diverting from Tolstoy's quote the prime form of adaptation of any Arab government should be simply that:

Not to seek power as through that only suffering will be caused. And Arabs cannot keep on suffering for no ones satisfaction of power.

VI.   [TACTICS AND STRATEGY]

As aforesaid the Arab world should keep peace with all yet be always prepared to fight. Supremacy demands a quote from Sun Tzu however as the approach of this book is significantly different I will add ten quotes from Machiavelli and on those expand the concepts of tactics and strategy of an Arab sovereignty.

1. "A prince never lacks legitimate reasons to break his promise."

A secular leader can't break consistency because that would break people's trust and the sovereignties strength as a whole. The leader must stick to his politics and the enhancement of the state so that the populous knows that whenever they want a certain value, they can get it from their state without disappointment.

2. "Before all else, be armed."

The Arab world is tricky and full of deceit. A friend is an enemy alike and the leaders of such a union or sovereignty must know their strengths, as their weaknesses and have their skills intact before attempting to attack or defend an attack. If Arab states fail to plan ahead of their actions, as well as their predictions of others actions they will very likely fail.

3. "I'm not interested in preserving the status quo; I want to overthrow it."

The leaders as well as their actions must inspire admiration and confidence. If their leader is the same as their past ones, then why should the populous come to you? Politics and leadership are a New and simultaneously old Game, a leader needs to give it new values, new rules in a new approach. The easiest way of leading a new market or a populous, or a unity is by inventing it.

4. "The end justifies the means."

Leaders should be result-focused rather than just busy. The populous will not accept their leader as secular, as liberal, as right, nor as effective if they do not witness constant benefits. Due to that it is only natural that great results, will lead to fortune. And great results demands creativity.

5. "Entrepreneurs are simply those who understand that there is little difference between obstacle and opportunity and are able to turn both to their advantage."

The actions of the leadership can be judged by the results of their problem solving. Every obstacle should appear to be an obstacle of the populous. An obstacle that was overcome for the good of the populous and the overall health of the Arab World will inevitably be to the advantage of the leadership and the secular growth of the sovereignty.

6. "Never was anything great achieved without danger"

Leaders should take calculated risks, as mentioned above, you need not fear failure. The faster they fail the better. Because every time anyone fails he falls, and one's low the only way is up. That is why we fall? To learn to pick ourselves up.

7. "Whosoever desires constant success must change his conduct with the times."

Keep track of your competitors and keep track of their leadership, what happens today might completely change tomorrow, that is politics after all. Know the principles of strategy; you need to constantly improve yourself. Gratification is the populous and their safety is the leader's priority.

8. "Where the willingness is great the difficulties cannot be great"

Leaders should know what they want and achieve it for the good of the growth of the territory. The Arab world cannot be restored to being the centre of the world if there are not determined liberal yet secular leaders that will be cunning and smart enough to play the games as is needed.

9. There is no avoiding war; it can only be postponed to the advantage of others.

In the Arab world that is for certain. One's war is inevitable postponement can only be to the advantage of the enemy. War should be placed under boundaries as I aforementioned so that it cannot be feasibly possible to create. But if it is, it should not be postponed.

10. "To understand the nature of the people one must be a prince, and to understand the nature of the prince, one must be of the people."

See problems and solutions from different perceptions. Understand your countries situation, and why people act the way they do.

VII.   [ADMINISTRATION]

I will not proceed to further detail. The administration of the Arab society should be vast, should be powerful should consist of a vast majority of the populous, secularism and libertinism. Through such the society as a whole can evolved.

The way the administration should be ruled should be following the same ten principles that I previously stated as tactics and strategy.

Only through such methods will success be granted.

The administration is liable for its actions. Peace, war, educational reforms, and overall reforms are part of the proper administration of the country.

By that I wish to state that the economic strength of the Arab world will not be a subject of the government in power but of the administration behind it. They should be responsible for investments, interior and exterior and the outcomes of such.

Furthermore the administration should be in charge of the internal security of the state. It should be administered by the government and there should be ideal yet appropriate sectors that will make sure it functions appropriately.

The administration should also be up to date with foreign politics and the potential influence this might have in domestic politics and international relations.

Finally I believe that that the administration is the back stone of any republic and must be used as such to create and maintain the purpose of what I would like to refer to the spiritual growth of the Arab world.

Much like every decent cycle of a functioning society the administration should be liable for international relations, domestic stability and enhancement of secularism. The administration should sufficiently appeal to the allies and make all enemies potential allies to prevent warfare.

The administration should also be aware of domestic problems and their outcomes as well as their solutions.

In an underlining account the administration ust hold the states objectives for the populous and the underlying values of an Arab political system.

If Arab leaders act in selfishness and refuse to give the administration any form of identification, methodological analysis and results it is inevitable in modernity that that state will survive long enough to progress but will instead be drawn back. A fine example of failed administrations can be seen from 1959 till today in Egypt. In 1959 all women in Egypt walked around with no hijab.

University pictures were taken without hijabs, society was more secular, every religion was accepted etc. The very fact that a bit over than half a century later this secularism and equanimity was lost states that progression has been backwards instead of forward.

Such examples are directly reasons to blame the administration, and any administration that inevitably causes steady retreat to ancient times rather than progressions to modernity. Finally, as was aforementioned if society goes back, politics and international relations can only follow.

VIII.   [INTERNAL SECURITY]

There is nothing more adamant about a city that has good arms as well as good laws. It is only rational that any society can look at the risk and dangers that lie before her and be able to engage when needed victory and deviate from the advantages and disadvantages of such discourse.

Internal Security is provided through various means. Means such as the army, which can keep stability and decline of extremism, laws that can be strictly dictatorial and be used to manage stability within the populous, furthermore, a strong police force, used as the first line of defence of the government before the use of the army can prevent any suspicious act. However, as these are complex systems that in order to be used need capability of planning, confidentiality, trust and cooperation, concepts are not particularly known over the Arab Republic I would suggest that internal security can be only maintained via what the world labels as seret services.

Internal security must primarily be indeed internal. No other foreign mercenaries, spies or whatever one might label them should interfere or be aware of the level of skill of internal mercenaries. That should be done to maintain success for foreign mercenaries whether training, or consulting the States internal security are usually led astray by missing the target, the training, refuse to produce what is necessary, or can easily turn against one's own.

Thus the leaders ought to personally choose the construct of their X internal security and it should be constructed of the republics own citizens. Experience can only uphold this choice for it has shown that the leaders and their republics, with their own army and their own internal security have done the greatest progress. Foreigners have only caused damage.

Once more one must draw a line. Modern politics calls that governments are much like conspiracies and if the Arab world turns into a conspiratorial power then its internal security will only proceed to do harm for the republic and its populous and not aid in the secular progression of the state.

With great confidence I will proceed to state of the political strategy that must take into account with the nation's internal security.

Primarily, the X bureau should under all circumstances be public. If privatized or privately funded its mercenaries will stop a secular approach to the countries internal security. Automatically, such a secret service is useless for its practitioners are frantically considered foreign mercenaries. And as foreign mercenaries they will go to the side of the highest bidder. And then what remains? The country is led into a highly unstable situation where their final and prime lines of defence have been sold and are governed by foreigners.

Where if internal security is a public matter, where it remains and struggles for the good of its populous nor will the society encounter issues such as that of the NSA nor will it fear its internal security for basically it will be the populous that will run it in cooperation with their secular leaders.

Internal Security is by far the most important theme of discussion. Secularism, progression and stability are concepts that cannot be discussed if domestic politics are unstable and internal security is weak.

The states should act in the best interest of the populous, and as such should behave in a manner, which will benefit the state. Accordingly, the sovereign of the state should not allow private interests to overrun public interest. The state through its internal security should progress to become a strong state as an organic whole, with the utmost control over its own domestic affairs as well as its foreign affairs.

 For, domestic affairs dominate the priority of the state and without domestic stability; the state cannot focus on international relations. In addition, the practice of diplomacy is essential for the state to maintain power and build a reputation on an international level. This aspect of international relations is a fundamental part of the survival and aggrandizement of the state, both on the political level and in terms of territorial control.

In essence then the confirmation of strong internal security is the only thing that can hold a state. Hold it in bonds of steadiness and immovability.

That being said in a state much like Russia where even the internal security is for the populous and follows the laws created by the state, thus it's something created for the people by the people the Arab Republic will be able to build strong economic bonds, deviate from extremisms and aid all forms and social groups.

With strong internal security the sovereignty can only progress steadily for the best.

Machiavelli defines the term "war craft" quite broadly. The idea encompasses more than just the direct use of military force. It consists of international diplomacy, domestic politics, tactical strategy, geographic mastery, and historical analysis. Internal security must hold the view of war as something that never could disappear completely, nor even conceive of the absence of war as a goal. Even in the most peaceful of times, the clouds of war always threaten.

VIII.   [EQUANIMITY, CONFIDENCE, AND ADVICE]

Equanimity is defined in Arabic as the evenness of mind, a calm temper which isn't easily elated or depressed and instead is patient, and leads with firm lack of disturbance by experience of or exposure to emotions, pain and other phenomenon that may cause the other to lose the balance of their mind. Essentially it is a concept very similar to Stoicism.

Others see equanimity as the need for self-exploration and emotional intelligence. A balance of everything if one likes.

Equanimity, confidence and advice tie in with a systemic study of Arab politics. If all these are used then fallacies will not emerge in the Arab World.

Wilson indicated four elements which comprise the character of constitutional states. These include:

 (1) representation of the people,

(2) administrative processes subject to the rule of law,

(3) a tenured judiciary, and

(4) formalized rights for individual liberty

Like the Athenians. Wilson believed a democracy could only be properly run by those trained and educated men heir to privilege, as long as their opportunity to rule was equal.

Thus equanimity in the Arab world can be identified to being equality and representation of the populous, a just legal system and judiciary as well as certain identified rights of the individuals (like the right to religion, to pray, to work, etc.).

The leaders that then run this Arab world must ensure to create the valued equinox for the populous. To establish equilibrium though such leaders as well as the populous should not simple practice their religious duties but surrender to this evenness of mind.

A Stoic approach to matters should be embraced by children from their first years in school, as well as the family as a whole.

Equanimity is so important as without that the balance of the Arab world would be much like that of today. There is no sign of cooperation, of remorse, forgiveness, unity and brotherhood, simply a fake adoption of religion just to ease the guilt of the actions of the Arabs. Most wars and murders have come in religious disguise and dogmatically accepted whilst if a true connotation of equanimity existed such cases themselves would have been condemned. Though the battle might have occurred it wouldn't be tied to religious causes and that by far, by itself is far more decent than the wars that have been tied with religious preaching.

All princes must build on strong foundations. The two essential components of a strong state are good laws and good armies. Good laws cannot exist without good armies. The presence of a good army, however, indicates the presence of good laws. All foundations must be built on equanimity, confidence and advice.

Nobility can be achieved by the grand public display of rewards and punishments. Above all, princes should win a reputation for being men of outstanding ability.

Therefore the leaders, the princes, the states equanimity and confidence must be built by the actions of the leader and the confidence of the populous grown towards the leader for his actions.

The state should encourage his citizens to excel in their occupations, and live their lives in peace. Thus, the state should never discourage or excessively tax private acquisition or prosperous commerce. Instead, the state should reward those who contribute to the overall prosperity of the state. Such rewards might include annual city-wide festivals and personal visits with guilds and family groups.

The advice allowed to proceed to the rulers of the state must then be simple when it comes to domestic and foreign politics.

For example the advice of the administration must be in account to the Balance of Power theory. When the state is about to witness war they must advice the leader on which side to ally with, which side is the strongest one to ally with.

For if the stronger ally wins, the leader of our state will be owed eternal debt, have acquired an interregional or international ally and be able thus to progress secularism and liberal thoughts as well as economic ties to benefit his populous. That itself will increase the confidence of the populous to their leader, and that will increase the overall equanimity of the state.

A leader of an Arab state should allow only wise advisers to speak with him, and only when he specifically requests their advice. The leader should not listen to anyone else and should be firm in his decisions. Vacillation will lead to a loss of respect whilst confident decisions, even if wrong ones, will increase the confidence of the populous and the stability of the state.

The leader must always seek advice, secular and liberal advice. But he must seek it only when he wants it, not when others thrust it upon him. Most important, a leader must always be cynical and sceptical about the advice he receives, constantly questioning and probing. If he ever discovers that someone is concealing the truth from him, he must punish that person severely. In the end, no matter how intelligent a leader's advisers might be, a leader is doomed if he lacks intelligence of his own. Wise leaders should be honoured for good actions proceeding from good advice.

Wise advisers must also be honoured but to an extent for if they are given too much power domestic balance can be dangerously interrupted.

A leader must fear, particularly when he is governing Arabs. If too much trust is shown to one adviser it is certain that the doom of the leader is near. A fine example of that is Mubarak and Sadat. Mubarak has been said to be the reason of death of Sadat. Full of conspiracy yet somewhat efficient if one notices the video of assassination.

One can battle with ignorance of his advisors, confidence of his people and equanimity of his state, and all of these might win. But by being vexed other the actions of their people leaders might fail to be capable to act for their people. At the end of the day a leader can only lead righteously a nation to the pages of history and international power by doing the right thing no matter how impossible or hard it may seem at times.

IX.   [FRAUD AND WAR]

The use of fraud is always magnificent and a glorious act when it comes to managing war. How so one may ask and the answer to that is rather simple. When one goes to hunt, the hunter, that is an image of war. Therefore the deception of hunters to the deer is itself a form of fraud. Rationally then the image of war and its outcome can be controlled by the deception. For if the deception is successful the deer might run away from what it perceives as an image and run directly into the image itself thus meeting its doom, or in other words success by the image of war.

Fraud in general terms is a despicable thing to do. To deceive one shows cunningness, lack of trust and ignorance. Yet in war it is perhaps one of the most important methods a state can adopt to be the successful image of war. When one state overcomes an enemy sovereignty by force it is a noteworthy victory. Yet if a state wins the image of war via deception it is equally praiseworthy, if not more than the use of force.

Fraud that breaks pacts and allies can acquire a state power and respect but never glory. Therefore, fraud must be used with an enemy that is untrusting. An enemy that can backstab you must be backstabbed first.

For example, the tragedy of Brutus and Julius Caesar, if both men are taken as sovereignties and images of war there was untrusting relations from the prime to the second but there was trusting relations from the second to the first.

Fraud and deception was righteously used by the prime since it was untrusting, but if the second image of war, Caesar killed Brutus it would have been documented as an act of violence, unjustified and Caesar would not hold the glory he has today in the pages of history.

In a more practical sense in modern society, cunning and deceit are traits and qualities that serve and individual better than force and abuse and from base will raise that individual to better conditions. It is part of the animal world and such actions can be noticed in a chameleon, which deceives, a frog, an alligator, a lion, and above all humans.

Machiavelli had stated the following:

If you only notice human proceedings, you may observe that all who attain great power and riches, make use of either force or fraud; and what they have acquired either by deceit or violence, in order to conceal the disgraceful methods of attainment, they endeavor to sanctify with the false title of honest gains. Those who either from imprudence or want of sagacity avoid doing so, are always overwhelmed with servitude and poverty; for faithful servants are always servants, and honest men are always poor; nor do any ever escape from servitude but the bold and faithless, or from poverty, but the rapacious and fraudulent. God and nature have thrown all human fortunes into the midst of mankind; and they are thus attainable rather by rapine than by industry, by wicked actions rather than by good.

*Hence it is that men feed upon each other, and those who cannot
defend themselves must be worried.*

Book III, Chapter 13

Fraud can be noted in modern times as well as in the Machiavellian era. Examples are best not to be used but can be found in the pages of our recent history and particularly through the word of mouth of conspiracy theories.

Fraud in warfare through proxy states is a modern method of warfare that is even more glorious then simple image deception for it causes the weak state to be ostracized by the populous, the international community and victims of a lost war

There are many ways to describe such victims but fraud as glorious as it is should remain in warfare. One might argue that international relations and international economic relations between nations are an image of war themselves, and that would be a righteous claim however when a state deceives another state for economic benefits the bubble inevitably bursts and such state is ridiculed internationally and even its own populous loses faith.

If it is used strictly in warfare then the country that firstly will use fraud, the country that will deceive the masses and the enemy by , for example financing arms spend of domestic terrorists whilst

condemning their terrorist actions and demanding war against this
terrorism is fighting an already victorious war.

All in all, deception unfortunately or fortunately is needed in war.
What exactly constitutes war is not something that one can respond
with a sufficient answer. War is the noose on the neck of certainty and
liberty, the inevitable agony and suffering of crying mothers who have
lost the national soldiers from a foreign bullet and the resulting
economic benefit for that country.

The image of war itself is fraud. Yet if fraud must be dealt with via
fraud it is by far a much more glorious act for a state to deal fraud via
fraud then fraud via force.

Deception is forgiven, force is remembered.

X. [THE PRESERVATION OF PEACE IN A REPUBLIC]

War and diplomacy are two key connotations in the foreign policies of a state. To create peace one must have over gone war and to preserve peace the state must not be in motion of another war.

The populous remains nothing more than malleable matter, gullible and subject to decisions of the leaders of the republic. Domestic peace, which is peace from wars within the republic, can be assured as long as the leaders of such a republic stay away from the property, the money and the women of the people. In war, or in any anarchical situation everyone will be forced to fight and protect what they have whilst in peace they will simply be content with what they already have and resist the chance of losing it.

Balance must be kept in the Arab world. A balance of virtue and detrainment of power for good will result from evil if such measures are not taken.

Good fortune of a republic, good leadership are elements upon which preservation of peace should be relied. Elements that themselves are unreliable, definable and subjects to change. Through them and other institutions such religions there must be an instillation of civic virtue.

However such unity and tranquillity of society is not one of value and purpose but one of satisfaction gained of interests and interest limiting being limited by the other.

Nevertheless, such peace is still a preserved peace from domestic mishaps. Society is run by special rules, objective universal laws which are only going to adapt by threat. If that threat is eliminated men will challenge and risk failure.

The only rationality is the rationality of individuals who can, by ridding themselves of pious illusions, control and form their own destinies. Humans can make their world by manipulating, controlling and dominating nature.

Not to deviate from the course of our subject and the nature of our topic to preserve peace the leaders must acknowledge that their world is created and lead by manipulating, controlling and dominating individuals and through such should be capable to employ the best of such nature from their own republic and place them forth in the first line of peace preservation of a republic, diplomacy.

In today's world one must acquire enough power as sovereignty to withstand the scrutiny of other nations. By that what I mean to say is that, if a country is as rich as Saudi Arabia for example, and as powerful as such, the violation of domestic human rights will not be acknowledged on an international level, nor scrutinized for being as such, simply because the international community cannot afford to upset a power such as Saudi Arabia.

Furthermore, sovereigntyshould rely on strong alliances to preserve peace. For if there is a balance of power between the aggressor and the defender then the aggressor will think twice before waging war and by such the defender will have the right to preserve its peace.

The nation state that is keen to preserve peace must be willing in many situations to "whore-out" to more powerful sovereignties. Much as in human relations to escalate from a lower position to a higher one one must experience total exoneration of values, beliefs, and honour such is the case with states. To preserve peace may simultaneously mean that an Arab state may have to surrender to its worst enemy, to give up all sentiments of value and all codes of honour.

To that I say that it is by far more significant that peace is preserved then if war is waged simply because of honour.

To that I say that it is to the interest of the Arabs to preserve and manage domestic and international peace, and preserve such peace under all circumstances. Unfortunately or fortunately, either way we do not stand in 15th century Florence. The world is by far more intertwined yet similar to 15th century Florence what cannot be explained and solved through politics usually resolves to war.

The solution to that is also rather simple. To avoid an escalation of politics to war, in other words avoid politics via war and preserve peace a clear cut agenda must be obtained and a political scorched earth policy.

The diplomats of such sovereignty must be efficient with excellent orating skills, capable to walk into any meeting, any gathering, any politically significant event with an agenda that serves best for their populous and destroying anything that the potential aggressor might use to escalate any situation into war.

Fundamentally and finally what is needed to preserve peace is determination and destruction of foreign interests in a regional war. For if interest is lost, for if interest is removed, or if interest is destroyed from the aggressor and their allies there will be no reason to wage war (other than domestic war, which that itself can be resolved as aforementioned) and thus the state will live a Spartan like successful govern-ship with peace fully preserved.

XI.   [EDUCATION AND THE STATE]

There is perhaps nothing that destroys education more than the institutions that serve it. As the New World Order is being finalized and as society progress to a totalitarian slave like unity the denigration of public education and public institutions in general is a noteworthy outcome compared to private universities who do not share this negative stigma of theoretically inferior facilities and a second-rate status.

In the Arab world then education must still remain a free secular prosperous thing, where the piece of paper gained by the individuals doesn't reflect a worthless title of an institution or the financial backup of the family.

Primarily then, such institutions should not take advantage of economic downturns to remove support from other universities and particularly public universities and raise tuition, privatize or cut back in the programs they offer.

Following that a state should not support recedes nor encourage such monstrosities such as student loans that automatically create a marker market for higher education. Students that come out of university with immense debt become enterprising sheep and rational consumers of educational products thus creating desperation for labour and cheap labour hands for employers.

The state should be funding every aspect of the university. It is absurd to have pharmaceuticals fund research assessment exercises to buy the morality of young doctors. It is absurd to have Law societies influence young lawyers as to what is justice and what is not. It is absurd to force politically different students think the way your faculty does. And finally it is absurd to, through the university; push one's own work to gain financial benefits off. These are all traits of states that lack virtue or lack leadership or perhaps both.

To attract the brightest minds then the Arab world must command the aforementioned traits.

Furthermore every unit of faculty in such universities should be one. Irrelevant as to whether they are part time or full time faculty members they should not feel vulnerable or affect the administration of the universities and disempower students and professionals alike. Such professionalism will inevitably enable attraction.

A university should not attract students with fancy pictures and titles. It should not have fantastic websites that promote antiracism, drinking, partying, and a two-to-four study units system.

One goes to University to work hard and gain knowledge beyond all else. All who seek to study at a University mainly for the title or to brag about their title should simply study in the appropriate institutions.

For in an Arab world the university should be based on the Bologna system. Not a mere collection of two or four subjects. Students should be challenged with eight or nine subjects per semester, languages, extracurricular activities, work placements, internships and whatever else one may.

Secularism should be promoted through such universities and the use of religious extremism should be prohibited. Once entering the university one should not be looked at for their religious believes, nor the colour of their skins but the decency of their character, that nature of their actions, their spiritual enlightment, and the amount of books they have read.

It is only wise to state that the university should be the states marvel. Should be adored, worshipped and protected. The Arab world must ensure that their universities are as magnanimous as the Western universities and should be sure they are powerful enough to challenge such universities.

Therefore all students should be entitled to a degree and there should be organized games between universities, domestic, Arabic and non-Arabic, as well as foreign and victories over foreign universities must be worshipped as victories over unfathomable facts.

For if an Arabic University proves to have a better debate team, a far more educated Model United Nations team then it is certain that through such acts it will arouse interest.

Furthermore, the state should ensure that its educational facilities have enough domestic sponsorship yet international agreements. It is, in today's world far more significant for an individual to finish with an undergraduate degree with attendance of courses in two or three universities rather than just one. It is for certain that an employer will worship greatly a degree and transcripts which label an individual as for example a BA in economics from the University of Tripoli, but with semesters in Harvard, MGIMO, LSE and other such noteworthy universities as well as work experience and field work.

Thus not only is the individual better educated for his purpose but has successfully attracted interest as being aware of numerous other nations, social and cultural norms. That itself should be a powerful consortium of factors which attract an employer.

There should also be no exemptions on entrance to a university. A university should not admit students based on just their grades, and financial situations. It is a rather astonishing embarrassment that educational faculties do that. The school system, particularly if one graduates from a school with an IB program is by far more knowledgeable than any other program.

That itself though should not be a reason for one with a public high school certificate not to attend a similar university. League rates and rankings are the prime reason for this. Universities are graded not on their level of education but on how many students they admit each year making it fundamentally only possible to those who could afford extracurricular activities and private lessons.

As a matter of fact universities should look not at their grades, but should interview such students and see, are they ready for university?

How determined they are to commit to their studies? Are they particularly fond of their studies? What extra knowledge they possess? Do they enjoy studying or do they merely do it because their mother demands it off them and forces them to do so.

These all are aspects that a university should consider. One does not get educated for a piece of paper. In the age of technology education is a choice, so is ignorance. One can be both, yet one can be none. It is an embarrassment if one choses the second over the prime.

But above all it is a disgrace to the very concept of education if one wants a piece of paper whilst he is marked by ignorance.

Book Four

I.   [ROLE OF THE MEDIA IN THE ARAB WORLD]

The Arabs have a wonderful combination of hating the West, yet worshipping it in many ways they refuse to see. For example, an Arab may condemn America, while wearing Levis jeans, smoking Marlboro and drinking Coca Cola. The only clear cut explanation of that is the role of the media in such states.

When a state is accustomed to live in freedom or has recently gained it, or is in seek of it, under its own laws, there are three ways of keeping it. The first one is to destroy it; the second is to go to live there in person and the third is to let it continue to live under its own laws, taking tribute from it, and setting up a government composed of a few men who will keep it friendly to you, traitors.

Now that method was the traditional method used by the Spartans and the Romans. Fantastic in use, particularly by the Romans who perfected such tactics, but in today's complex political system more indirect methods have to be used. In today's world for example the destruction of Iraq has only brought despise to the occupier but not friendlier approaches. To live in it would mean dealing with inevitable guerrilla warfare by groups such as the Hezbollah and to take tribute from it would label you as the international Pimp, blocking many gateways to international relations on the international basis.

Therefore the two ways one can dominate a state, and particularly a state that is Arab based is through its media. Arabs generally enjoy music, music videos, movies, news, and all that. It is not necessary for the Arabs to be westernized, but to seem that they have been.

In essence then the media will lie, as every media in the world lies and adjusts news to a modernized Western accepted connotation so that the Arabs can sympathize with it.

The role of the media though should not be that in the Arab Republic. On the contrary the media should stand secular and honest. It should inform of the plans of the governments, pros and cons. Be a method of expanding knowledge therefore there should be debates aired, a viral sharing of knowledge and appreciation for the populous.

The media's role in this society is fundamentally a function of how this society chooses to use the media. Will it be a tool of information and spiritual enhancement or abusiveness of western based ideologies and those of companies. Furthermore, the media's relationship with this society is both reflexive, the mass media simultaneously should affectand affected by society.

The role of the media is also partially in the hands of the people. t's important that media consumers not be passive; rather, they need to be constantly active. Instead of just "absorbing" media content like sponges, consumers should be constantly asking themselves and others questions about the media. Thus in an Arab Republic there must media controlled religious, political, and economic secularity that doesn't simply breastfeed the populous with information but causes them to think and expand their thought whilst simultaneously destroying aforementioned biases, racist concepts and others of such ill-natured.

II.   [SOCIAL GROUPS]

Social groups are perhaps the best defence of society against a rogue republic. One has only to look at America and Facebook activism to know that social groups are capable of igniting resistance, revolution and unity.

Fundamentally Social Groups in an Arab Republic should:

- Solve problems in society and the community as a whole
- Raise Awareness on corruption and political decay
- Develop methods to sustain the youth from extremism in ways such as friendly games, discussions and what may that prevents the rise of fundamentalism and extremism but expresses an overall unity and happiness
- Pursue, discuss and create new opportunities to engage with citizens and non-governmental sectors.

Social groups can either be products of the system they were born to destroy or an altruistic escape of society. Social groups are vital for the Arab world. One can only look at the Egyptian and Tunisian revolution. Social media was the key, the spark that ignited a war against tyranny. The outcome of course was unfathomable tyranny that followed but nevertheless the overthrow of long-term autocratic governments in Tunisia and Egypt, the battle by rebels to defeat the 42-year rule of Muammar Qadafi in Libya and the civilian unrest in Syria and Bahrain calling for democratic change: all of this represents the biggest change in Arab politics for decades. In progress we realized that this war is really a war on terror. The element of social groups stands in retrospect against the outcomes of the revolutions.

For example the internet is useful for news gathering and social media for connecting and co-ordinating groups and individuals. Mobile phones for taking photographs of atrocities to share for the wider global audience but what happens if those are simply blocked?

The Egyptian government's decision to cut all communication systems, including the internet and mobile phones, on the night of 27 January was widely perceived to be a watershed moment in the overthrow of the Mubarak government.

Yet the revolution proceeded. Social groups have a general bonding which is undignified by the government for some reason. For examples members of social groups can understand hidden messages from handshakes, songs, actions, fundamentally everything.

Therefore I believe that in the Arab world social groups should be given the liberty of the west. If the X social group turns to extremism it should be in the interest of all the other social groups to abolish it from existence. In parliament and in society in general it is best to have all opinions out in the open however in the case of a developing republic and on the grounds that that republic is aiming to progress spiritually and socially they must depend on secularity and destruction of far right or far left ideas. Society as a whole must stand on the centre of the spectrum and develop that way.

Therefore, in my own opinion then social groups are like the kryptonite of society. They are there for good, and can cause immense benevolent good if they are run properly, much like many trade and worker unions that could help workers and traders if they were not run by corruption themselves.

The social groups that will form reflect strictly the cultural norms of the society and reflect the amount of corruption in its government. If the government is not corrupt and struggles to fight corruption in a society where itself does ostracize any symbol of corruption or malevolent usage and abuse of structure then the social groups that are in fact part of the society will only exist to enhance the success of the state.

III.   [LITERARY AND PHILOSOPHICAL WORK]

As I am by all means not worth mentioning great mathematical masterpieces this section of my work will lie only for the science which I have studied, worship and above all live by and that would be philosophy, literature, politics and law.

The works that address society are extremely important, for they mould society, raise it, give it values and ethics. For a strong society like the Arabic one I would highly recommend the following list:

- The Persians
- Philoctetes (Aeschylus)
- Phrygians (play)
- Prometheia
- Prometheus Bound
- Prometheus Pyrkaeus
- Prometheus the Fire-Bringer
- Prometheus the Fire-kindler
- The Danaides (Aeschylus)
- The Danaids (Aeschylus)
- The Eumenides
- The Libation Bearers
- The Sphinx (Aeschylus)
- Meditations on First Philosophy
- The Wealth of Nations

- Leviathan
- Electra (Euripides)
- Nicomachean Ethics
- The Republic
- The Origins of Totalitarianism
- (Rousseau) Social Contract
- On Liberty
- Metaphysics of Morals
- The Art of War
- The Art of War (Machiavelli)
- Discourses on Livy
- Machiavelli's Prince
- Human, All Too Human
- The Communist Manifesto
- The Kreutzer Sonata
- The House of the Dead (novel)
- Humiliated and Insulted
- Notes from Underground
- The Gambler
- Death and the Dervish
- The Idiot
- The Crucible
- Anna Karenina
- Journey to the Center of the Earth
- Waiting for Godot
- War and Peace

- Around the World in Eighty Days
- Divine Comedy
- To Kill A Mocking Bird
- The Brothers Karamazov
- Death of a Salesman
- The Great Gatsby
- A Christmas Carol
- David Copperfield
- The Hunchback of Notre-Dame
- Dr Jekyll and Mr Hyde
- A Tale of Two Cities
- The Count of Monte Cristo
- Othello
- Odyssey
- 20,000 Leagues Under The Sea
- Oliver Twist
- 1984 - George Orwell
- Macbeth
- Hamlet
- Anne Frank: The Diary of a Young Girl
- The Kite Runner
- Crime and Punishment
- The island
- V for Vendetta
- The Da Vinci Code

The reason why I proposed a sample of the works I would suggest that a healthy sample of a republic should read are works which I have personally read myself. The list of course is infinite and the sample I proposed is only a percentage of the books I have in mind. Perhaps if I was wiser than the average individual I would have more to add. These works are works I have personally read and through them I have experiences wisdom, bravery, heroism, death, love, anger, theory, spiritual enhancement among many more sensations. But those basic sensations are sensations that I firmly believe that every individual in a healthy state should read and be aware of to the extent that social understanding itself evolves if such readings are done. To this I have come by encountering a very brave man who could have easily studied law, or philosophy yet his commitment to language, literature and linguistics show a medieval like chivalry and commitment that does not exist in many men whilst in reality it should have existed in all men.

IV.   [FINAL THOUGHTS]

There are many more things that one can say. Many more dreams and aspirations, views and opinions that can be expressed and attempted to be silenced as has been the case with many brave men before me. As a man who lives and practices Machiavellianism at its fullest from everyday encounters to university and works such as this I can only express how I feel reality is.

Reality for the Arabs then is that having perhaps a United Arab Republic or a Middle East Union is a complicating matter which is complicated simply by individual and social hunger to strive for self-improvement. It is in the nature of the Arab to be a good host but it is not in his nature to connect too much. There are a few exceptions like myself who do not always encounter everything for profit.

But the Arab World for example when imposed with its biggest threat, the war with Israel it united yes, but united as different sovereignties and not as one power. All countries that fought held their own grounds, their own plans, plainly none cared about the actions of the whole that would potentially be destructive to the enemy.

Of course I do not intend to attack Israel, which is not my point. In this era internationalism and politics are more complicating than what they seem. Perhaps the best benefit for the region would be to make friends of old enemies and enemies of friends, or perhaps maintain equilibrium. I cannot be definite cause the Arab world across its history has not been predictable, but simple chaotic.

The way I see it though, perhaps the biggest challenge is to finally leave religious extremism behind and become a one united power, perhaps then it would be the strongest power the World has ever seen. Dreams remain dreams, and this book is just a vision, not meant to offend any individual, any state, any sovereignty or any leader.

Arabs should not fear poverty and death, they should worship them and live their life in an attempt to be Stoic. To live and love all their world with smartness and political kindness.

www.ingramcontent.com/pod-product-compliance
Lightning Source LLC
Chambersburg PA
CBHW070747290526
45795CB00002B/505